QUALITY QUOTES BY RATAN TATA - THE 'ANMOL RATAN' OF INDIA

DR DHEERAJ MEHROTRA &
LUCKNOW MANAGEMENT
ASSOCIATION

Made with ♥ on the Notion Press Platform
www.notionpress.com

Ratan Tata, a legendary industrialist from India, has long been an anchor in the country's economic landscape. His illustrious family hails from Mumbai, and he presided over Tata Sons and the Tata Group from 1990 to 2012 and 2016 to 2017. Winner of India's highest civilian honours, the Padma Vibhushan (2008) and Padma Bhushan (2000), with congratulations,

Tata is well-known for his charitable work and his involvement with the Indian startup scene. He had a hand in a number of the landmark purchases that brought this esteemed company group into the contemporary age and made it more competitive, including Tetley, Jaguar Land Rover, Corus, and Air India.

Contents

Foreword

Ratan Tata's conversations over the years have offered countless pearls of wisdom, reflecting not just words but the essence of his character—both in his personal and professional life. The world would undoubtedly be better if even a fraction of his insights were internalized and practised. Dr Dheeraj Mehrotra has done an admirable job of capturing and sharing many of Tata's impactful words for the benefit of all.

Writing the foreword for this remarkable compilation, Quality Quotes of Ratan Tata, India's Anmol Ratan, is a privilege. This book, curated by a distinguished education professional, captures the wisdom, insights, and timeless values of one of India's most revered figures, Ratan Tata. His words are not merely expressions but reflect a lifetime of experience, character, and conviction—qualities that have shaped him as a visionary business leader, a compassionate philanthropist, and a true nationalist.

Ratan Tata's journey has been a testament to leadership driven not by the pursuit of wealth but by an unwavering commitment to integrity, humility, and a deep sense of social responsibility. As a business leader of unparalleled competence, Tata has not only built one of the most respected and diversified business empires in the world, but he has also infused it with a set of core values that stand as a beacon of ethical corporate governance. Under his stewardship, the Tata

Group has become synonymous with trust, fairness, and innovation—qualities that reflect the man himself. However, not merely his business acumen sets Ratan Tata apart. What truly distinguishes him is his profound humanity. Despite his immense success and influence, he is remembered and respected not for his wealth but for his character, compassion, and dedication to the service of others. In a world often driven by profit and power, Ratan Tata is a quiet, strong and humble figure. He has always believed that businesses have a more significant role to play in society than just generating profits. This belief has been reflected in his philanthropic endeavours, which range from education and healthcare to rural development and technological innovation. His often-understated generosity has transformed countless lives and uplifted entire communities, embodying the true spirit of giving back to society.

Ratan Tata's legacy is not merely the result of the business empire he created but of the values he championed. His often simple yet profound quotes are a window into a mind that values ethical conduct, commitment to excellence, and empathy for humanity. His guidance has inspired generations of entrepreneurs and business leaders and touched the hearts of ordinary individuals seeking to impact their communities positively. His words are about business success and living a life of purpose, honesty, and a deep sense of duty to one's nation and fellow citizens.

In this compilation, Dr Dheeraj Mehrotra has done a commendable job selecting and presenting a treasury *of Ratan Tata's thoughts. The reader will find here a source of inspiration, a guide for ethical living, and a call to embrace the higher ideals that Ratan Tata has always embodied. The book is not just about quotes—it is about absorbing the essence of a life well-lived, a life dedicated to the betterment of society, and a life that teaches us that true greatness lies not in accumulating wealth but in enriching the lives of others.*

As you turn the pages of this book, you will be reminded of why Ratan Tata is India's 'Anmol Ratan'—a priceless gem who has consistently led by example, guided by principles of fairness, humility, and an unwavering commitment to the greater good. I hope this book will glimpse his extraordinary life and inspire readers to imbibe and act upon the values he dearly cherished. Ratan Tata's legacy continues to shine through his achievements and the enduring impact of his words and actions. This legacy will continue to inspire generations to come. May this book be a source of strength and guidance to all who seek to lead with integrity, act with compassion, and live with purpose.

October 28, 2024

A.K. MATHUR, Sr. Vice President LMA

Preface

Ratan Tata, an iconic figure in India's industrial landscape, has left an indelible mark through his visionary leadership and humble persona. His words have always been a beacon of wisdom, offering insights into life, business, leadership, and philanthropy. This compilation, **Quality Quotes by Ratan Tata - The 'Anmol Ratan' of India**, is a tribute to the man whose impact goes far beyond the business world.

Tata's quotes encapsulate his unwavering commitment to integrity, excellence, and humility. As the former chairman of Tata Sons, he transformed the conglomerate into a global powerhouse and upheld the ethos of ethical business practices and social responsibility. His thoughts on leadership, innovation, risk-taking, and empathy serve as life lessons for generations to come.

This book is curated to inspire individuals—entrepreneurs, leaders, or young minds—who seek wisdom from one of the finest minds of our times. It is a humble attempt to bring to light the profound simplicity of Ratan Tata's thoughts, which continue to resonate deeply in a world in constant flux.

I hope these quotes will motivate readers and give them the clarity to navigate their journeys, whether in business or life, with the grace and grit that Ratan

Tata exemplifies.

Let these words be a guiding light for all who aspire to make a difference.

Dr Dheeraj Mehrotra In Association with Lucknow Management Association (LMA)

"Never underestimate the power of kindness, empathy, and compassion in your interactions with others." This quote highlights Tata's belief in the importance of human connection and compassion.

Prologue

Ratan Naval Tata was born in Mumbai, India, on December 28, 1937, and died on October 9, 2024, at 86. He was a distinguished Indian industrialist and philanthropist. From 1991 to 2012, he was the Chairman of Tata Sons, the holding company of the Tata Group, during which time he led the conglomerate to new levels of success and global recognition. Under his stewardship, the Tata Group expanded its international presence, diversified its portfolio, and became synonymous with innovation and excellence across various industries, including steel, automobiles, telecommunications, and hospitality.

Ratan Tata's most significant accomplishments include the acquisition of global brands such as Jaguar, Land Rover, and Tetley and the introduction of the Nano, the world's most affordable automobile. In addition to his business acumen, he is acknowledged for his dedication to sustainable development and social responsibility, as evidenced by his involvement in the Tata Trusts, which prioritise healthcare, education, rural development, and poverty alleviation. Ratan Tata's legacy as one of India's most influential figures in contemporary history has been solidified by his extensive admiration and numerous accolades generated by his visionary leadership and unwavering dedication to business and societal advancement.

• xvi •

ONE

QUALITY QUOTES BY RATAN TATA

———❦———

"

"Don't wait for opportunities to come to you, create your own opportunities."

"Power and wealth are not two of my main stakes."

"Businesses need to go beyond the interest of their companies to the communities they serve."

"What I would like to do is to leave behind a sustainable entity of a set of companies that operate in an exemplary manner in terms of ethics, values and continue what our ancestors left behind."

"Take the stones people throw at you and use them to build a monument."

"The day I am not able to run the company successfully, I will take the decision to step down."

On Innovation & Growth:

"I admire people who are very successful. But if that success has been achieved through too much ruthlessness, then I may admire that person, but I can't respect him."

"A new India must be created – an India of modern industries. And enterprises must be created by Indians."

"I have been constantly telling people to encourage people, to question the unquestioned and not to be ashamed to bring up new ideas, new processes to get things done."

"Challenges need to be given to an organization."

"The strong live and the weak die. There is some bloodshed, and out of it emerges a much leaner industry, which tends to survive."

On Character & Values:

"Apart from values and ethics which I have tried to live by, the legacy I would like to leave behind is a very simple one - that I have always stood up for what I consider to be the right thing."

"Don't be serious, enjoy life as it comes."

"Integrity and honesty are absolutely essential for success in life - all areas of life."

"If it stands the test of public scrutiny, do it... If it doesn't stand the test of public scrutiny then don't do it."

"The joy of doing something comes from peoples' appreciation of your work."

On Success & Failure:

"I don't believe in taking right decisions. I take decisions and then make them right."

"Success and failure are both part of life. Both are not permanent."

"Difficulties and hardships are just opportunities in disguise."

"If there are challenges thrown across, then some interesting innovative solutions are found. Without challenges, the tendency is to go on the same way."

"All of us do not have equal talent. But all of us have an equal opportunity to develop our talents."

On Personal Growth & Attitude:

"Sometimes your best investments are the ones you don't make."

"The day I am not able to fly will be a sad day for me."

"I've often made bold statements myself to force a decision."

"A person who is trying to copy others will be a failure."

"Life is like a game of cards. We cannot change the cards that are dealt to us, but we can surely play them to the best of our ability."

On Nation Building & Society:

"We need to focus on making India a better place to live in, not just to invest in."

"I believe India has huge potential, and the time has come to actualize it."

"Young Indians are not afraid to step out of their comfort zones."

"India happens to be a rich country inhabited by very poor people."

"What we need to do is to give young people opportunities to help them grow."

On Corporate Leadership:

"The job of leadership is not to spread pessimism but to spread optimism."

"Profitable is not enough. It has to be profitable with a conscience."

"People still believe in the Tata Group's value system."

"I have always been bullish about India's potential."

"Good leadership involves responsibility to the welfare of the group."

On Innovation & Change:

"Change is not always comfortable, but it is essential."

"I would say that one of the things I wish I could do differently would be to be more outgoing."

"There are many things that, if I have to relive, maybe I will do it another way. But I would not like to look back and think what I have not been able to."

"The future belongs to those who believe in innovation."

"Don't limit your challenges; challenge your limits."

On Business Philosophy:

"Business is not just about making money, it's about making dreams come true for others."

"A company's worth is also measured by the way it conducts its business and keeps its promises."

"Employees are a company's greatest asset - they're your competitive advantage."

"I would say that if you are not being ethical in business, there is no point in being in business."

"The most important thing is that we as a group stand together."

On Vision & Ambition:

"I don't believe in making right decisions, I make decisions and then make them right."

"The strong live and survive and the weak die and fade away."

"Nothing worthwhile is ever achieved without deep thought and hard work."

"If you want excellence, you must aim at perfection."

"I have been constantly telling people to encourage people, to question the unquestioned."

On Management & Leadership:

"Management is all about managing in the short term, while developing plans for the long term."

"Take the stone people throw at you, and use it to build a monument."

"The best way to destroy an enemy is to make him a friend."

"If there are challenges, there must be ways to overcome them."

"Lead by example, not by instruction."

On Personal Values:

"Real excellence and humility are not incompatible with each other."

"I may have hurt some people along the way, but I would like to be seen as somebody who has done his best to do the right thing for any situation."

"We live in an increasingly competitive world, and we need to be prepared for that."

"None can destroy iron, but its own rust can. Likewise, none can destroy a person, but their own mindset can."

"Life is like a game of cards. The hand that is dealt you represents determinism; the way you play it is free will."

On Growth & Development:

"I am not a person who wants to look back on my career."

"The trouble with a lot of business leaders is that their compass points to money, power, fame and glory."

"Growth has to be profitable and profitable has to be with a conscience."

"You have to see failure as the beginning and the middle, but never entertain it as an end."

"Cultivate the habit of listening, not just hearing."

On Social Responsibility:

"We need to make a difference not just for the company but for the community."

"Wealth does not mean anything if it doesn't benefit others."

"Business needs to go beyond the interest of their companies to the communities they serve."

"What you create should be of service to the people."

"We must continue to build trust with the community we serve."

On Success & Achievement:

"Take risks in your life. If you win, you can lead; if you lose, you can guide."

"I admire people who are successful, but if that success has been achieved through too much ruthlessness, then I may admire that person, but I can't respect him."

"Success is not a destination, but a journey."

"The ones who are crazy enough to think they can change the world are the ones who do."

"Achieving success is hard, but sustaining it with dignity is harder."

On Learning & Growth:

"Learning from mistakes and constantly improving products is a key in all successful companies."

"Your attitude is more important than your capabilities."

"Experience is what you get when you don't get what you want."

"The best preparation for good work tomorrow is to do good work today."

"Knowledge is like a garden; if it is not cultivated, it cannot be harvested."

On Innovation & Future:

"The future depends on what you do today."

"I don't believe in pressuring people. When you pressure people, you don't get the best out of them."

"We have to find innovative ways to break the cycle of poverty."

"Innovation is not about saying yes to everything. It's about saying NO to all but the most crucial features."

"Technology is going to define the future of business."

On Life Philosophy:

"Life is not just about existence, but about what you do with that existence."

"The beauty of life doesn't depend on how happy you are, but how happy others can be because of you."

"Don't take yourself too seriously. Take your commitments seriously."

"Problems are best solved when you address them rather than avoid them."

"The purpose of life is not just to be happy, but to matter."

Final Wisdom:

"A sustainable business is one that lives in harmony with the environment."

"Good intentions might sound nice, but it's positive actions that matter."

"Light will always triumph over darkness."

"Be humble in your confidence yet courageous in your character."

"The difference between ordinary and extraordinary is that little extra."

On Perseverance & Determination:

"A person's true character emerges in times of crisis."

"Don't be afraid to take big steps. You can't cross a chasm in two small jumps."

"The one constant in life is change. Embrace it."

"Dreams are not what you see in sleep, they are the things that don't let you sleep."

"Hard times don't create heroes. It is during the hard times when the 'hero' within us is revealed."

On Business Innovation:

"I have always been driven by the desire to create something new."

"In a competitive world, not taking risks is the biggest risk."

"A business model that hasn't evolved in decades needs disruption."

"You cannot build a great business on a weak foundation."

"Quality is not an act, it's a habit that needs constant nurturing."

On Leadership Style:

"Lead with empathy, not just authority."

"The best leaders are those who know how to follow."

"Your legacy is defined by the lives you touch, not the wealth you accumulate."

"Leadership is about inspiring others to dream more, learn more, do more."

"A true leader takes responsibility for failures and shares credit for successes."

On Personal Development:

"Your preparation for tomorrow begins with your choices today."

"Comfort zones are beautiful places, but nothing grows there."

"What you hear is opinion, what you see is perspective, what you feel is reality."

"Judge yourself by what you can do, not by what others cannot."

"Every milestone reached should be a starting point for the next journey."

On Vision & Progress:

"Yesterday's solutions won't solve tomorrow's problems."

"The cost of inaction is greater than the cost of making a mistake."

"Look at problems as opportunities in work clothes."

"A vision isn't just a picture of what could be; it's an appeal to our better selves."

"Progress is impossible without change, and those who cannot change their minds cannot change anything."

On Building Trust:

"Trust, once broken, takes more than time to rebuild."

"Your word should be your strongest currency."

"Credibility is built over decades and can be lost in moments."

"People invest in trust before they invest in business."

"Relationships are like glass. Sometimes it's better to leave them broken than hurt yourself trying to put them back together."

On Corporate Culture:

"Culture eats strategy for breakfast."

"The workplace should be where people feel valued, not just employed."

"Create an environment where people want to belong, not just work."

"Your team's growth is your growth."

"A company's culture is the foundation of its future."

On Innovation & Adaptation:

"The world belongs to those who see possibilities before they become obvious."

"Innovation is not about technology; it's about solving problems."

"Don't wait for the perfect moment; take the moment and make it perfect."

"The only way to predict the future is to create it."

"What worked yesterday might not work tomorrow."

On Social Impact:

"Profit should never come at the cost of human values."

"A business that makes nothing but money is a poor business."

"The impact of your work should outlive your time."

"Success is meaningless if it doesn't contribute to social good."

"True wealth is measured by the lives you've touched."

On Resilience & Adversity:

"The strongest steel is forged in the hottest fire."

"Obstacles are stepping stones to success."

"In every adversity lies the seed of opportunity."

"Your response to failure matters more than the failure itself."

"Challenges are not meant to break you, but to make you stronger."

On Business Ethics:

"Ethics and profits are not mutually exclusive."

"Good business is where profit meets principle."

"Short-term profit should never compromise long-term reputation."

"The right way might be harder, but it's always worth it."

"Your conscience should be your first board of directors."

On Personal Growth:

"Each day is a new opportunity to be better than yesterday."

"Knowledge without action is like a book that's never read."

"Your growth is measured by how you handle success and failure."

"The difference between a good decision and a bad one is timing."

"Learn from everyone, follow no one."

On Leadership Wisdom:

"A leader's job is to elevate people, not eliminate them."

"Authority comes from character, not position."

"The best form of leadership is leading by example."

"Great leaders create more leaders, not followers."

"Leadership is about making others better because of your presence."

On Future Thinking:

"Plan for tomorrow but live for today."

"The future belongs to those who prepare for it today."

"Innovation comes from looking beyond what exists."

"Every ending is just a new beginning."

"Change is inevitable, growth is optional."

On Decision Making:

"Sometimes the right decision isn't the popular one."

"Decisions made in anger are rarely good ones."

"When in doubt, choose growth over comfort."

"Time is the best teacher for decision-making."

"Every choice you make makes you."

On Professional Excellence:

"Excellence is not a skill, it's an attitude."

"Quality means doing it right when no one is looking."

"Your work speaks louder than your words."

"Perfection is not attainable, but excellence is within reach."

"The difference between ordinary and extraordinary is practice."

On Building Relationships:

"Trust takes years to build, seconds to break, and forever to repair."

"Business is about people, not just profits."

"The strongest partnerships are built on mutual respect."

"Your network is your net worth."

"Good relationships keep good businesses alive."

On Innovation & Creativity:

"Don't follow the crowd, create your own path."

"Innovation comes from questioning the status quo."

"Creativity thrives under constraints."

"The best ideas come from solving real problems."

"Think beyond the obvious."

On Personal Values:

"Your character is your destiny."

"Integrity has no price tag."

"Success without values is no success at all."

"Your reputation is your most valuable asset."

"What you stand for is more important than what you gain."

On Opportunity & Growth:

"Every obstacle is an opportunity in disguise."

"Growth happens outside your comfort zone."

"The biggest opportunities often come from solving the biggest problems."

"Success isn't about avoiding failure, it's about learning from it."

"Don't limit yourself by others' limited imaginations."

On Team Building:

"A strong team can make any vision a reality."

"Talent wins games, but teamwork wins championships."

"Hire character, train skill."

"The strength of the team is each individual member."

"Great things are never done by one person."

On Business Strategy:

"Strategy without execution is just theory."

"Think long term, act short term."

"Markets change, good values don't."

"Competition makes you better, not bitter."

"Focus on value creation, not valuation."

On Personal Development:

"Your attitude determines your altitude."

"Knowledge increases by sharing, not saving."

"What you learn must translate into what you do."

"Yesterday's methods won't solve tomorrow's challenges."

"Growth and comfort rarely coexist."

On Achievement:

"Dreams don't work unless you do."

"Success isn't owned, it's rented - and rent is due every day."

"The journey is as important as the destination."

"Small progress is still progress."

"Achievement lies in the effort, not just the result."

On Entrepreneurship:

"Start small, dream big, but most importantly, start."

"Entrepreneurship is not just about starting a business, it's about solving problems."

"Risk comes from not knowing what you're doing, not from the action itself."

"A good idea without action is like a car without fuel."

"The best entrepreneurs think beyond profit."

On Leadership Evolution:

"Leadership is a privilege, not a right."

"True leaders create an environment where others can succeed."

"The measure of a leader is not command, but inspiration."

"Leadership is about making people believe in themselves."

"Great leaders are also great listeners."

On Professional Growth:

"Your career is what you make of it."

"Professional growth happens when preparation meets opportunity."

"Skills can be taught, but attitude must come from within."

"Your work ethic determines your worth."

"Experience is the name we give to our mistakes."

On Business Philosophy:

"Business must have a purpose beyond profit."

"Sustainable success comes from sustainable practices."

"Market leadership is earned, not bought."

"Quality remembers long after price is forgotten."

"Good business serves society first."

On Personal Excellence:

"Excellence is not a destination; it's a continuous journey."

"Your biggest competitor should be yourself."

"What you do when no one is watching defines who you are."

"Reputation takes a lifetime to build, minutes to destroy."

"The difference between good and great is attention to detail."

"I don't believe in work-life balance. I believe in work-life integration. Make your work and life meaningful and fulfilling, and they will complement each other."

Tata is one of the most employee-friendly companies in India, and there is no doubt about that because Ratan Tata believes in the policy of being answerable to the employees as well. He shared, "As a business leader, you have to face your shareholders.

"

TWO

THE RATANS OF
RATAN TO INDIA

"Take the stones people throw at you, and use them to build a monument."Tata's resilience and ability to turn adversity into opportunities is a testament to his character.

Presenting the 25 significant contributions of Ratan Tata to India:

1. Tata Nano Project
- Introduced the world's most affordable car at Rs. 1 lakh
- Aimed to make car ownership accessible to middle-class Indian families
- Revolutionized automotive engineering with innovative cost-cutting solutions

2. Acquisition of Jaguar Land Rover (2008)
- Put India on the global automotive map
- Saved thousands of jobs in the UK
- Transformed the brands into profitable ventures

3. TCS Growth
- Transformed Tata Consultancy Services into India's largest IT company
- Created hundreds of thousands of jobs
- Made India a global IT powerhouse

4. Tata Daewoo Acquisition
- Marked India's first major international automotive acquisition

- Enhanced India's commercial vehicle manufacturing capabilities
- Expanded global footprint of the Indian automotive industry

5. Indian Hotel Industry Development
- Expanded Taj Hotels globally
- Set new standards in Indian hospitality
- Preserved iconic properties like the Taj Mahal Palace, Mumbai

6. Tata Steel's Global Expansion
- Acquisition of Corus Steel
- Made Tata Steel a global player
- Created one of the largest steel manufacturers in the world

7. Education Initiatives
- Established various educational institutions
- Provided scholarships to thousands of students
- Supported research and development in multiple fields

8. Healthcare Contributions
- Built cancer hospitals
- Supported medical research
- Made treatment accessible to underprivileged sections

9. Rural Development Programs
- Initiated various rural development projects
- Supported farmers through technology and training
- Created rural employment opportunities

10. Disaster Relief Work
- Provided immediate assistance during natural disasters
- Helped in rehabilitation efforts
- Supported affected communities long-term

11. Tata Teleservices
- Helped revolutionize the Indian telecom sector
- Made communication accessible to the masses
- Introduced innovative services

12. Environmental Conservation
- Promoted green technology
- Implemented sustainable business practices
- Supported environmental conservation projects

13. Employment Generation
- Created millions of direct and indirect jobs
- Promoted skill development
- Supported entrepreneurship

14. Women's Empowerment
- Promoted gender equality in the workplace
- Supported women entrepreneurs
- Created special programs for women's education

15. Innovation Promotion
- Established R&D centers
- Supported startups
- Promoted Indigenous technology development

16. Sports Development
- Supported various sports initiatives
- Built sports facilities
- Sponsored talented athletes

17. Cultural Preservation
- Preserved historical monuments
- Supported arts and culture
- Protected India's cultural heritage

18. Defense Manufacturing
- Contributed to India's defence capabilities
- Created Indigenous defence technologies
- Promoted Make in India in the defence sector

19. Ethical Business Standards
- Set benchmarks for corporate governance
- Promoted transparency in business
- Established ethical business practices

20. *Infrastructure Development*
- *Invested in roads and bridges*
- *Developed ports and airports*
- *Contributed to urban development*

21. *Digital India Initiative*
- *Supported the government's Digital India program*
- *Promoted digital literacy*
- *Invested in digital infrastructure*

22. *Social Entrepreneurship*
- *Supported social enterprises*
- *Promoted sustainable business models*
- *Created social impact through business*

23. *Agricultural Innovation*
- *Supported farmers through technology*
- *Promoted sustainable farming practices*
- *Invested in agricultural research*

24. *Financial Inclusion*
- *Made banking services accessible to rural areas*
- *Promoted micro-finance initiatives*
- *Supported financial literacy programs*

25. Philanthropy Through Tata Trusts
- Largest philanthropic organization in India
- Supports various social causes
- Invests in community development projects

These contributions have helped India's economic growth and made a significant social impact. Ratan Tata's vision of ethical business practices and social responsibility has set a benchmark for corporate India. His leadership transformed the Tata Group from a largely India-centric organization to a global conglomerate while maintaining its core values and commitment to social development.

ᐅᐅᐅ

THREE

Lessons Learnt from Ratan Tata

"I admire people who are very successful. But if that success has been achieved through too much ruthlessness, then I may admire that person less."This quote highlights Tata's emphasis on ethical business practices and human values.

Along with emphasizing ethical leadership and social responsibility, the lessons that may be learnt from Ratan Tata's journey provide a thorough roadmap for success in one's personal and professional life. Through his economic understanding and commitment to humanitarian causes, he developed a distinctive approach to leadership that has endured the test of time.

He placed such an emphasis on persistent education, which is evidence that success is not a destination but rather a journey. Even though he had achieved great success, Tata continued to teach himself about business and technology to adjust to the shifting times. This approach was evident in his decisions to buy foreign companies such as Jaguar Land Rover and Corus Steel, demonstrating how learning and flexibility go hand in hand.

He knew that long-term success is always the result of a group effort, as seen by the emphasis on trust-building and collaboration. Under his direction, the Tata Group was not only concerned with the brilliance of its members but also with establishing an environment in which all members could contribute and develop. Using this strategy, the organisation could become a global powerhouse while preserving its fundamental principles.

It is also significant that he had a mindset towards accepting risks. Although the debut of the Tata Nano was not a commercial success, it demonstrated his willingness to take risks to accomplish a more significant societal objective. The connection between this and his emphasis on vision demonstrates how large aspirations, when matched with social good, may drive entire organisations to push the frontiers of what is possible.

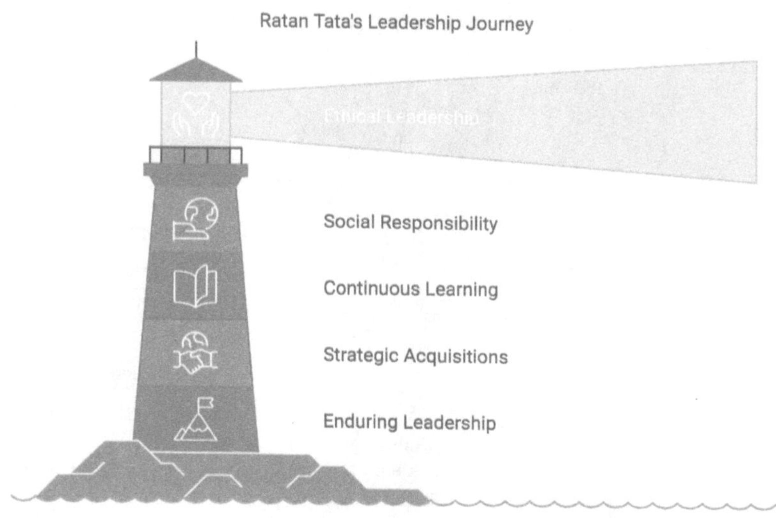

Perhaps most crucially, what differentiates Tata from many other corporate executives is that he focused on empathy, compassion, and giving with a purpose. It was not enough for him to simply write checks; instead, he strived to make a long-lasting influence through his philanthropic work. The Tata Trusts' work in education, healthcare, and rural development demonstrates how a company's commercial success can benefit society.

It is clear that leadership is not only about managing what already exists; instead, it is about actively crafting a better future. This is demonstrated by seeking responsibility, being innovative, and being inclusive. Through Tata's legacy, we learn that genuine success is not in what we accomplish for ourselves but in what we make possible for others to achieve.

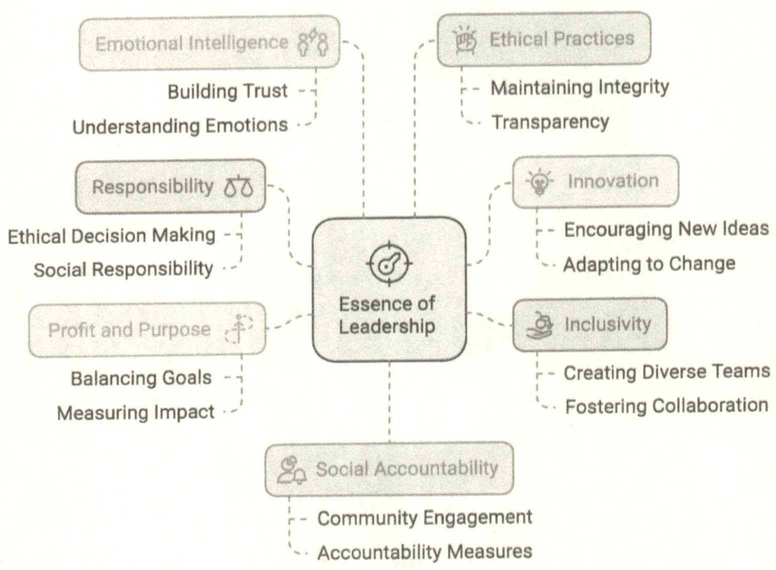

These teachings are particularly pertinent today because organisations increasingly need to balance profit and purpose, and leadership involves strategic thinking and emotional intelligence. Ratan Tata's ideas provide a framework for achieving this equilibrium while upholding ethical standards and social responsibility.

▷▷▷

FOUR

A note on Ratan Tata's Leadership Style

Tata's emphasis on building strong teams and empowering others is a hallmark of his leadership style.

Beyond doubt, Humility, approachability, and a focus on people were the defining characteristics of Ratan Tata's leadership style:

Focus on the people

Tata was well-known for its employee engagement, which included listening to employees' thoughts and problems, connecting with employees at all levels, and developing a sense of belonging. He firmly believed in giving employees autonomy and the authority to participate in decision-making.

Through his acts and behaviour, Tata established a high standard for others to follow. He exemplified the work ethic, integrity, and values he demanded from others.

To successfully manage shifting business

conditions and trends in the industry, Tata demonstrated adaptability, which encouraged flexibility and creativity.

Socially responsible

Tata championed programs and efforts that benefit society and incorporated social responsibility into his approach to leadership.

A humble person

Not only did Tata demonstrate that leaders do not have to be loud, boisterous, or bullying, but he also demonstrated that his leadership style was humble and meek.

Tata was an Indian industrialist and philanthropist who transformed the Tata group from a household name in India to a brand recognised worldwide.

Ratan Tata's Leadership Style

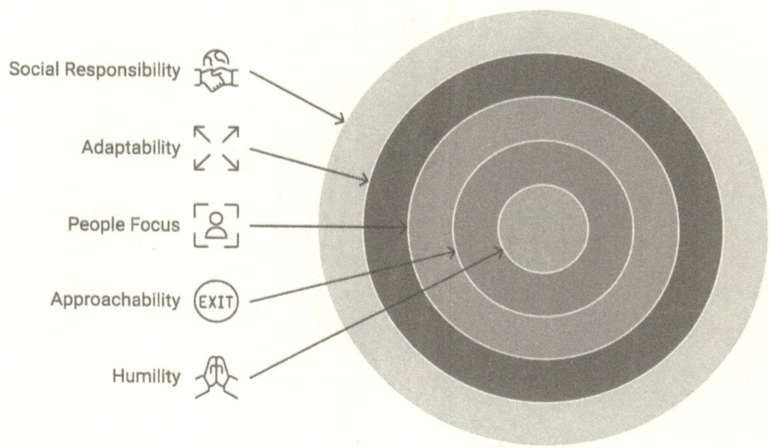

"

ᘐᘐᘐ

FIVE

ICONIC PHILANTHROPIST

"Don't wait for opportunities to come to you, create your own opportunities"

Iconic philanthropist and visionary leader Ratan Tata was a well-known figure.

In addition to being synonymous with business success, Ratan Tata was also a figure who stands out as passionately committed to society's welfare. As a pioneer in corporate philanthropy, he was made famous by his conviction that firms had to prioritise giving back to society more than they should on merely pursuing profits. His efforts concentrated on meaningful humanitarian causes, ranging from education and healthcare to crisis assistance and animal welfare. Tata's leadership stretched beyond boardrooms; he was active in various organisations.

Ratan Tata formed the Taj Public Service Welfare Trust in response to the crisis that occurred after the terrorist attacks in Mumbai in 2008. This initiative was developed to help those affected by the catastrophe, demonstrating Tata's empathy and dedication to assisting individuals impacted by disasters. It is also laudable that he showed leadership during the COVID-19 pandemic by donating Rs 500 crore to assist India in its fight against the virus. This demonstrates his commitment to serving the public good further.

As part of the Tata Group's commitment to education and healthcare, Ratan Tata ensured that sixty-five per cent of the company's income was made available to charity trusts. Through their efforts in crucial sectors like rural development, education, and healthcare, these trusts were able to make a significant and long-lasting impact on the lives of millions of people. His work revealed that multinational firms could be agents of social transformation.

Tata's compassion extended beyond the well-being of humans to the welfare of animals. The global headquarters of Tata Sons, Bombay House, was constructed to provide a safe haven for stray dogs. This seemingly insignificant yet profound act demonstrated that he cared deeply about all living things.

Mentorship for Young Entrepreneurs Ratan Tata expanded his sphere of influence by providing young entrepreneurs with mentoring, direction, and the opportunity to benefit from his vast professional experience. Tata empowered the next generation of leaders by mentoring them and encouraging entrepreneurship and appropriate business practices.

A Strong Moral Compass is the Foundation of Tata's Approach to Philanthropy. Tata's approach to philanthropy was founded on profound moral principles. He believed that philanthropic work ought to be guided by ethical principles of right and wrong, primarily emphasizing enhancing society's conditions and addressing urgent problems.

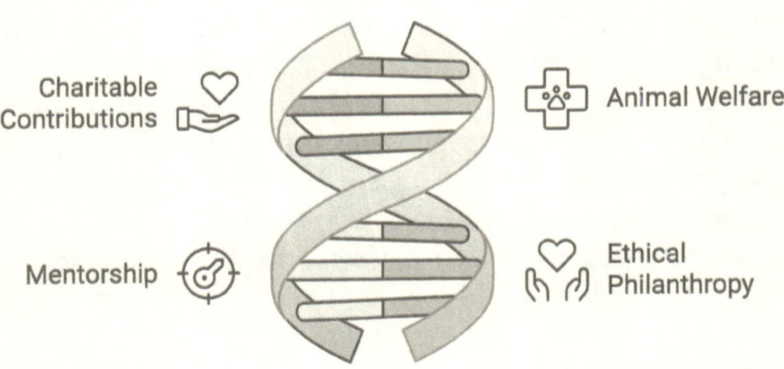

SIX

Ratan Tata and his Values

"The only way to win is to not be afraid of losing."

During his tenure as Chairman Emeritus of the Tata Group, Ratan Tata was renowned for his unwavering commitment to morality and honesty.

His core beliefs include the following:

Tata exemplified the work ethic, ethics, and ideals he expected from others by setting an example for others to follow.

He actively engaged with staff representing all levels of the organisation, listening to their thoughts and concerns.

He ensured his employees' efforts were recognised and rewarded because he respected their contributions.

In terms of excellence, he emphasised the importance of the Tata Group continuing to push the boundaries of innovation and perfection.

A humble attitude. He believed that it was necessary to remember one's roots and origins and the sacrifices one's family had made for them.

Authenticity. He exemplified the virtue of integrity, which stands out as the most essential aspect of his *character.*

Be willing to take criticism. His motto was, "Collect the stones thrown at you by the people and use them to build a monument." He greatly emphasised working together and collaborating with others' efforts.

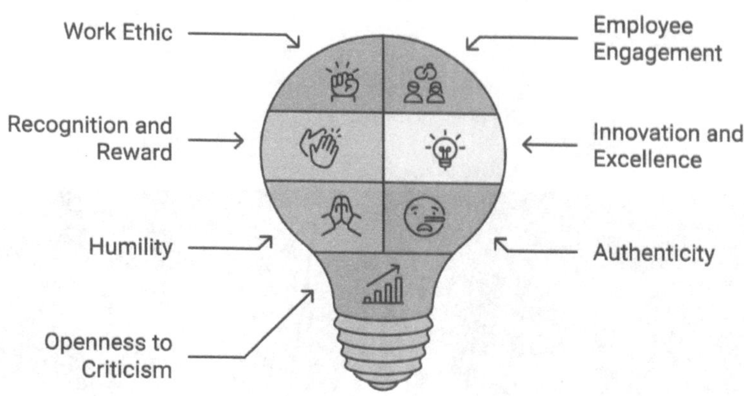

ᗪᗪᗪ

SEVEN

INSPIRATIONAL STORIES

The only limit to your success is your own imagination

Ratan Tata was renowned for his unshakeable devotion to morality and honesty throughout his stint as Chairman Emeritus of the Tata Group. He was particularly well-known for this commitment.

His fundamental convictions consist of the following:

To demonstrate the work ethic, ethics, and principles that he anticipated people to possess, Tata acted as a model for others to emulate.

He actively interacted with staff members representing all levels of the organisation, listening to their opinions and concerns and involving himself in the conversation.

He ensured his staff members' efforts were acknowledged and recognised to show his appreciation for their contributions.

Building a Morally Strong Organization

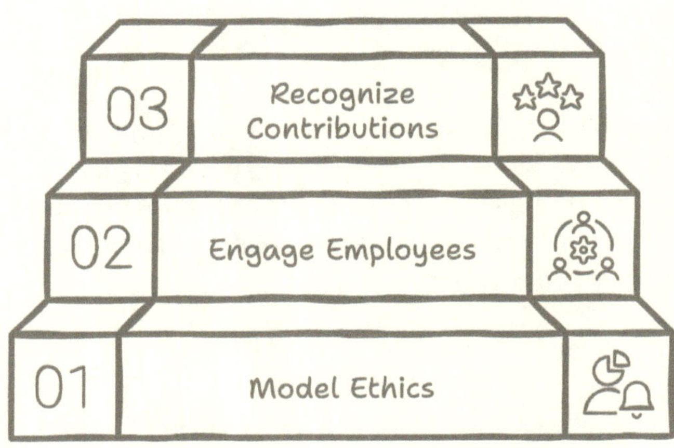

Specifically, he underlined the significance of the Tata Group continuing to push the limits of innovation and perfection to achieve excellence.

He had an attitude of humility. He considered it essential to remember one's roots and origins and the sacrifices one's family had made for them.

One's genuineness: He was a shining example of the virtue of integrity, which stands out as the most essential feature of his character.

You should be open to receiving feedback.

His principle of action was, "Collect the stones thrown at you by the people and use them to build a monument." He highlighted the need to work together and partner with others' efforts to a considerable extent.

❧❧❧

• 64 •

EIGHT

25 LEARNINGS FROM RATAN TATA

"What I would like to do is to leave behind a sustainable entity of a set of companies that operate in an exemplary manner in terms of ethics, values and continue what our ancestors left behind."

1. *Vision and Leadership: Establishing Transparent and Prolonged Objectives*
- Consider the long-term implications of your actions.
- Set an example for others to follow - Strike a balance between innovation and tradition -

2. *Develop successful business concepts. The two pillars of business ethics are maintaining the highest ethical standards, never compromising on beliefs, building trust via openness, keeping pledges and agreements, and prioritising reputation over short-term gains.*

3. *The Innovation Approach: Fostering Creative Thinking with Encouragement*
- Learn from your mistakes - Take chances on a calculated basis
- Adapt to the ever-changing times - Concentrate on real-world problem solutions

4. *Managing people and recognising the value of human capital*
Strong teams should be built.
- Foster talent - Conduct promotions based on merit - Establish environments that are welcoming to all

5. *Responsibility to the Community*
It is important to give back to society, consider the impact on the community, support educational programs, concentrate on sustainable development, and address social issues.

6. *Individual Growth and Development*
- *Never stop gaining knowledge - Remain modest despite your achievements*
Work-life balance should be maintained.
- *Develop your habit of self-discipline - Continue your professional development*

7. *Making decisions: Think strategically; take into account the long-term repercussions; strike a balance between the risks and the benefits; seek the counsel of experts; and have faith in your gut instincts*

8. *The Expansion of Businesses*
- *Be on the lookout for chances - Make provisions for long-term growth*
Establish a presence on a worldwide scale while upholding quality standards.
Put the demands of the consumer first.

9. *Managing a crisis requires you to maintain composure in high-pressure situations, confront issues head-on, and gain wisdom from adversity.*
Take care of the team's spirit and come up with creative solutions.

10. *The Nature of Leadership*
These are all important requirements, including being approachable, listening to all stakeholders, delegating well, empowering people, and leading with compassion.

11. *A culture of innovation that fosters the development of new ideas, supports research and development, embraces technology, encourages creativity, and rewards innovation*

12. *Establishing solid alliances and maintaining stakeholder relations*
Honour pledges and uphold the principle of transparency
- Make sure that everyone comes out ahead. Relationships must be valued.

13. Establishing a Brand
- Put an emphasis on quality; - Establish trust; - Ensure maintaining consistency; Generate value; - Consider the long term

14. Risk Management: *Conduct thorough evaluations, make contingency plans, monitor closely, learn from your mistakes, and always be ready for anything.*

15. A Perspective on the World
- Think globally; - Show respect for different cultures; - Construct bridges; - Establish networks; - Uphold professional standards

16. The Welfare of Employees
- Make safety a top priority - Incorporate possibilities for advancement
- Ensure that compensation is equitable - Encourage a healthy balance between work and personal life
- Foster an atmosphere free of negativity

17. A Focus on the Shopper
- Recognise the requirements; - Provide value; - Preserve quality; - Foster loyalty; - Exceed the expectations of the customers

18. *An obligation to protect the environment*

By setting an example, promoting sustainability, reducing impact, innovating solutions, supporting conservation, and leading by example

19. Financial management should include cautious planning, prudent investment, the maintenance of reserves, cost control, and the guarantee of transparency.

20. Standards for Quality Twenty: Maintaining consistency, setting high benchmarks, monitoring regularly, and continuously improving are all important. Never make concessions -

21. Capabilities in Communication: Be understanding; listen attentively; communicate information; maintain connections; and cultivate partnerships

22. Task prioritisation, effective planning, meeting deadlines, respecting the time of others, and maintaining organisation are all aspects of time management.

23. Problem-Solving: Conduct Thorough Analyses, Think About Your Options, Take Decisive Action, Keep Track of Your Results, and Gain Knowledge from Your Experiences

24. Team Building: Make a thoughtful selection, train consistently, and motivate efficiently. Build trust, and Rejoice in your accomplishments.

25. Legacy Planning: Establishing Institutions, Developing Leaders, Creating Systems, Transferring Knowledge, and Ensuring Continuity

These insights reflect Ratan Tata's comprehensive approach to business and life, which emphasizes the significance of striking a balance between successful corporate endeavours and social responsibility, as well as personal development and organizational advancement. His approaches continue to serve as a source of motivation for company executives and entrepreneurs worldwide.

NINE

The Retirement That Wasn't – Tata's Role as an Influencer

After Ratan Tata retired as Chairman of Tata Sons in 2012, he exemplified how influential leaders could continue making substantial contributions outside their formal roles. Shifting from a corporate leader to a visionary mentor and philanthropist, Tata embraced his new role with dedication and purpose.

Several aspects defined Tata's post-retirement journey:

1. Investments in Businesses

He actively invested in promising ventures, focusing on innovative solutions and developing sustainable business models. Tata became a crucial figure in India's startup ecosystem by supporting young professionals and promoting digital transformation.

2. Philanthropy

He took charge of the Tata Trusts, where his leadership was dedicated to addressing pressing social issues, advancing education, supporting healthcare initiatives, and fostering rural development across India. Through these efforts, Tata's impact reached millions, enhancing the quality of life for underserved communities.

3. Mentorship

Guiding new entrepreneurs, Tata shared invaluable business knowledge, offered strategic advice, encouraged innovation, and championed ethical practices. His mentorship left a profound mark on the next generation of Indian business leaders.

4. Societal Impact

Through his ongoing commitment to community development, Tata promoted sustainable growth, supported environmental initiatives, and advocated for social entrepreneurship. His legacy of societal contribution continued to positively shape India's future.

Ratan Tata's journey post-retirement reaffirmed his belief that success was not solely about personal achievement but about creating a lasting, positive impact on society. He remained a significant force through his ongoing involvement in business and philanthropy, inspiring future leaders to blend business success with social responsibility.

TEN

LEGACY AND LASTING IMPACT

Through his legacy, Ratan Tata has left behind a blueprint for ethical leadership and sustainable growth. Among the business impacts are the following:

1. The transformation of the Tata Group into a global powerhouse; the establishment of benchmarks for corporate governance; the demonstration of successful international acquisitions (JLR and Corus); the creation of world-class Indian brands; and the establishment of sustainable business practices.

2. Creativity and having a vision: In addition to promoting research and development, embracing technical advances, encouraging entrepreneurial thinking, and demonstrating a long-term vision, Tata Nano was a pioneer in the field of cheap technologies.

3. Contributions to society include Philanthropic Leadership, strengthening the influence of Tata Trusts, focusing on sustainable development, supporting education initiatives, promoting accessibility to healthcare, and investing in rural development.

4. Community Development. This initiative has created employment possibilities, promoted social entrepreneurship, supported skill development, and resolved societal concerns.

5. Promoted inclusion in the growth process. Principles of Leadership. Maintained the highest possible level of honesty - Encouraged openness - Constructed trust via actions - Exhibited a significant level of corporate responsibility - Established industry standards

6. An approach centred on people, places a high value on human capital, encourages inclusive growth, supports employee development and creates happy work environments.

7. Established powerful groups of people. India's global reputation has been enhanced, Indian managerial qualities have been demonstrated, international relationships have been built, cultural understanding has been promoted, and global possibilities have been created. These factors have contributed to India's dominance on the worldwide stage.

8. Standards for the Industry: In addition to establishing quality standards, promoting environmentally responsible corporate practices, demonstrating ethical business conduct, and encouraging innovation, the industry has Established reputable brands.

9. A lasting impact on the business world through:

The establishment of quality standards;

The promotion of global thinking;

The demonstration of sustainable growth;

The demonstration of the value of innovation;

The inspiration for ethical business practices;

10. The Next Generation: Young entrepreneurs who have been inspired, who have promoted the culture of startups, who have demonstrated social responsibility, who have encouraged innovation, and who have demonstrated the importance of values

11. In the social sector, the philanthropic sector has been strengthened, strategic giving has been promoted, sustainable effect has been demonstrated, and social innovation has been encouraged and demonstrated the significance of measurement.

12. Implications for the Future: The evolution of business, with an ongoing emphasis on innovation, a focus on resource conservation, the significance of morality, a global point of view, and a Responsibility to the community.

13. Development of Leadership Skills: Leadership is founded on values, such as thinking about the long term. An emphasis on innovation - An approach that is people-centred - A social consciousness awareness

There is much more to Ratan Tata's legacy than just his business success. He has demonstrated that achieving business success and being socially responsible are not mutually exclusive. By placing a strong emphasis on ethics, innovation, and social effect, he has established a new paradigm for business *leadership. His influence continues to be felt today through the countless organisations, activities, and individuals he has inspired.*

His road proves that true success is not just about building successful businesses but also about positively influencing society while adhering to the most excellent ethical standards. This all-encompassing approach to leadership and social responsibility motivates and directs subsequent generations, making his legacy timeless and increasingly relevant in today's complex world.

The Master's Voice

Be a person of integrity, and always do what is right, even when it is difficult.

Books By The Same Author

www.authordheerajmehrotra.com

About Lma

LMA has a huge multidisciplinary resource base among its individual and institutional members, which is comprised of distinguished professionals. It leverages this valuable resource in its various programmes.

VISION

A high profile, vibrant body of professionals contributing to making UP Uttam Pradesh. One of the top in India, with a permanent representative on the national apex body-AIMA

MISSION

We sensitize and catalyze individuals, institutions and communities to actualize their potential. To create and sustain a movement of professional management in and around Lucknow by reaching out to working and future managers and facilitating their participation and involvement in the proliferation of principles and practices of management.

VALUE

We are equal among equals. We believe in involvement, commitment and mutual respect.

BELIEF

Build the Dreams, Repeat the Dreams and the Dreams Build you up.